THE ART OF THE

JAPANESE GARDEN

THE ART OF THE JAPANESE

By TATSUO ISHIMOTO

GARDEN

CROWN PUBLISHERS, Inc.

NEW YORK

FOR KIYOKO

© 1958 by Crown Publishers, Inc.
Library of Congress Catalog Card Number: 58-8314
PRINTED IN THE UNITED STATES OF AMERICA

Seventh Printing, January, 1964

Table of Contents

Introduction

This new book is the result of a five-month tour of Japan during which I visited gardens in villages, towns and cities from one end of Japan to the other. In all I shot more than 2,000 photographs in these gardens. I talked to garden-owners, garden-designers, garden-workmen, plant-growers.

My plan was to gather ideas for American gardeners. I would see and photograph the celebrated Imperial and Temple gardens, but I would also visit private family-gardens. I would seek out the lovely, quiet, private, intimate gardens hidden from the street by fence or wall or hedge, seldom seen by visiting tourists.

These small family-gardens interested me most of all. For in these, I felt sure I would find the ideas most useful to Americans—the structures and plant groupings, the pathways and fences, the stone and water arrangements. As the months went on, my idea proved right. And in this book you will find that most of the photographs present the Japanese family-garden. This book also is, to my best knowledge, the first such presentation of Japanese family-gardens ever made available in English for use by Westerners.

The art of garden-making is honored in Japan as in no other nation. It is almost literally true that *everyone* in Japan loves gardens. Every family, wealthy or humble, has its garden. Or if not a complete garden, at least some planting, some treasured and cared-for reminder of nature. There is nothing new or recent or modern about this, although there are "modern" Japanese gardens and we shall see some of them in later pages of this book.

The beginnings of garden-making and garden design in Japan go back many centuries. The early steps of development are obscure, but it is certain that an interest in gardens and garden design was included in the stream of cultural ideas which crossed the China Sea to Japan from the Chinese mainland twelve and more centuries ago.

In ancient Japan garden-making slowly took on a character of its own, departing sharply from the Chinese. The distinctive character of Japanese gardens was well established ten centuries ago, and it is fair to say that Japan's gardens today have behind them a thousand years of continuity.

What is the special character of the Japanese garden? It cannot rightly be summed up in a word, but if any one word is most nearly appropriate, the word is *natural*. These are natural gardens.

By this I do not mean that Japanese gardens are literal copies of nature; they are not. Rather, they are reminders of nature; really appreciations of nature. But over the centuries the garden-maker has learned to achieve his natural effects with few and simple materials, to suggest, to hint, to edit and to eliminate.

There are numerous misconceptions about Japanese gardens. Let me mention one or two.

Misconception one: that Japanese gardens always follow certain rigid rules with regard to both arrangement and content. This is not true at all. Classic plans for "hill gardens" and "level gardens," for stone arrangement, for bridges and pathways, for tea gardens—all these do exist and are followed. But the garden-maker today works with a relatively free hand. Many newer gardens show the results of experimentation. Many also show the influence of contemporary Western architecture and landscape architecture. The important thing is not that the Japanese garden-maker follows rules, but that tradition and the experience of centuries guide his hand.

Misconception two: that Japanese gardens are miniature gardens. This is simply not so. Perhaps this curious idea caught on through confusion with the Japanese art of the *bonsai*, the miniature tree-landscapes grown in containers. Perhaps it stemmed from the fact that many Japanese gardens (including many in this book) are very small. But even in a small Japanese garden, nothing is in miniature. The plants are not always dwarfs; the bridges and pathways are designed for full-size adults.

Occasionally in Japan one sees what appear to be effects in miniature. These are exceptions and are quite contrary to the basic philosophy of Japanese garden design.

Perhaps one reason for pinning the term *miniature* onto Japanese gardens is the matter of scale. All of Japan, to Western eyes at least, may appear to be in reduced scale. The average height of the Japanese is less than that of the Westerner. Houses are modular in design and the module used (usually 36 and 72 inches—the dimensions of the *tatami* floor mat) is small to American eyes. Distances between villages and between cities are short. Another surprise in Japanese gardens is in the limitation of color. American friends of mine who have never visited Japan confess that their ideas of Japanese gardens have come to them from their awareness of Japanese flowering trees and of Japanese flower arrangements. Aren't Japanese gardens, therefore, ablaze with flower color?

Nothing could be further from the truth. Basically, Japanese gardens are evergreen gardens. Certain shrubs and trees may flower in season. And a cutting garden for flowers may exist. But the gardener will often shear away the flowers on a shrub in the course of pruning; the shape of the shrub is the important thing. And the cutting garden may be tucked away somewhere out of sight.

A note on bamboo

These giant woody grasses so popular in Japan grow very well in those parts of the United States where winters are mild. The giant timber bamboo can survive in temperatures as low as 15 degrees; other varieties can stand a low temperature ranging from 28 degrees for the unusual black bamboo down to 5 degrees for the palmate bamboo.

If you grow your bamboo in large containers—tubs, boxes, or pots—you can often ignore the hardiness limitation. Grow the bamboo as a perennial and protect its roots in winter.

The Japanese frequently use bamboo as a material to screen one part of the garden from another part, or to screen the garden from the street or from neighboring gardens.

Your nurseryman can suggest trees that will do a similar screening job for you. Don't be afraid to plant closely or to prune trunks to achieve a clean, vertical line.

You might consider using any of the following trees for screening: white birch, poplars (if you have the room and can accept the great height they reach at maturity), yews and other vertical trunked conifers (you can plant these closely and prune their side branches), and willows in many forms.

The Japanese also use bamboo as a structural material. They make fences with it; they even use it as water pipe. Unfortunately, in much of the United States bamboo poles are fairly expensive and not easily available.

Bamboo gives a natural effect when used in fencing and garden structures. For a similar feeling, you might consider using unfinished redwood, red cedar, or cypress. These woods weather naturally and beautifully, and deteriorate very slowly.

Other hardy substitute trees

Among other hardy plants that will give you effects similar to those in the photographs are amur maple *(Acer ginnala)*, a hardy, good substitute for Japanese maple; flowering dogwood (any of several varieties) to be used as the Japanese use flowering fruit trees; and Catalpa *(Catalpa bignonioides)*, a hardy tree used as a single specimen tree. The Umbrella Catalpa is a dwarf form useful in a small garden.

Stone

In the United States, a different kind of stone is available in each area, and it is usually both wise and economical to use a local material. Stone that is weathered, rounded, river-washed, moss- or lichen-covered is preferable to stone that is quarried, split, or machine-cut.

A note of acknowledgment:

Numerous people in Japan were most helpful to me in preparing this book. While space will not permit mention of them all, I should name a few without whose help the book would not have been possible. Among them are Eijiro Nunokawa, Motonosuke Shibata, landscape architects, and Kodo Matsubara, architect; and especially Shinichi Maesaki, an old friend who understands Japanese gardens well and taught me a good deal. I also should thank Japan Air Lines for facilitating my travels throughout the Japanese islands. All of the photographs in this book were made with a Minolta Autocord camera.

Japan is a beautiful country

Japan is a beautiful country. Crowded as it is, over half of the land area is still forest-covered. And no matter where you are, close to you is the sea.

It is written that the Japanese live with "one foot in the sea." In this mountainous island country, most people dwell on the alluvial plains along the coasts, with mountains rising behind them and the sea at their doorstep.

Mountains dominate the landscape. Down their slopes rush many swift streams and rivers, cascading in waterfalls, pausing in hillside pools and small lakes. The mountains are not only forested, they are rocky.

In the high mountains are stands of fir, larch, hemlock, spruce—also azaleas, dwarf bamboo, dwarf birch and dwarf pine. On the lower slopes grow oak, elm, magnolia, also linden, birch, cherry—all trees familiar to Americans

although the species differ from the native species of the United States.

In the lowlands are the gardener's favorites—black pine and red pine and the tall bamboos.

And always, not far away, is the sea. The coastline is indented, particularly on the Pacific and on the Inland Sea. The eye takes in sea and plain and steeply rising mountains in a single glance. You see man's works—in town and temple—and nature's forms and colors existing together in harmony.

This is the natural aspect of Japan. This is the "nature" that lies at the heart of Japanese garden design. When a man looks out from the living room of his house into his small garden, he is reminded of mountains and their forest cover, of a mountain stream, and perhaps of the sea nearby. Thanks to his garden, the peaceful reassurance of nature will not escape him even in the heart of the city.

Silver Pavilion *(Ginkaku-ji)* in the ancient garden city of Kyoto. One feature of this garden is the flat-topped cone of sand which suggests Mount Fuji and also, in the evening, appears as a silver moon when viewed from above.

Japanese families travel ... and study gardens

Wherever one goes in Japan he encounters families on tour. They visit temples and temple gardens, historic shrines, mountain lakes. Like Americans, they are camera enthusiasts. And they enjoy photographing the famous gardens.

Arched bridge in Imperial Garden in Kyoto. Notice detailing on the bridge rail, and the pole decking.

The Jigsaw bridge is typical. This kind of bridge is much more fun to cross than a straight plank bridge, and much more interesting to look at.

Black pine garden on the Japan Sea. These trees like salt air and sandy soil. Note the open fence in the background.

The Ryoan-ji rock garden in Kyoto is perhaps Japan's most famous. No trees or shrubs, just raked sand and large stones. It suggests the sea.

The stone lantern (Ishitoro) is used today primarily for decoration, but in older gardens the lanterns were also important sources of light.

Garden pathway in Nikko. Note the collection of lanterns at the right. Note also the irregularity of the paving stones.

Garden gate in Nagoya. The gable roof is typical, also the open bamboo fencing. Beyond is an azalea garden in flower.

Garden gate in Kyoto, much simpler in style—just two upright posts. Notice the careful placement of the steppingstones.

Steppingstones in the famous Heian Jingu garden, Kyoto. The interest here is the irregular placement, which makes crossing an adventure.

Stone pathway approaching the Ishiyama shrine near Kyoto. Even with cut materials, the Japanese carefully avoid too rigid a design.

The famous public gardens are full of ideas

Properly the photographs here should show Japanese fathers and mothers walking the paths, children crossing the steppingstones or posing for photographs. I made my pictures when the gardens were empty only because I wanted the ideas and designs to show more clearly.

These are the gardens tourists see—American tourists and Japanese tourists. The Japanese, particularly, come not only to appreciate beauty but also to study the art of garden-making. Here are ideas to take home.

The arching bridge in Sadatoshi Kawamura's garden. Except for the man-made bridge, this appears to be a natural scene. Yet the garden, when photographed, was only four years old!

(Opposite) A pathway through pebbles in the famous Katsura garden, built by Prince Toshihiko in 1602.

What makes a Japanese garden?

The idea comes first, then the materials. The garden-maker may wish to suggest a woodland, with a mountain backdrop. He may want the splash of a waterfall, or the murmuring sound of a stream flowing over pebbles. Or he may dispense with water if he wishes, using stones to suggest a stream-bed.

Study the photograph opposite, then turn the page for a close-up of some of the elements in the tool kit of the Japanese garden-maker.

Privacy from the street—the garden-owner wants to shelter himself from the curious glances of passers-by. Here he uses a neat bamboo fence mounted above a low wall.

A welcome to guests. The garden gate with its wing fences says "welcome" and clearly shows the way into the garden. Note the planting along the pathway.

The stone bridge. Here natural slabs form the walkway. The large stones on either side warn the stroller to take care. They also deflect the course of the water below.

Bamboo forest. These large bamboo leave the garden floor uncluttered. The same effect can be achieved with birches, but more space is needed.

The garden pathway. The stones make walking interesting and keep strollers off the moss ground-cover. Note the borders of inset stone, also the guards of bent bamboo.

The garden gate. This simple gate looks at home in the garden. Note the easy, loop gate-latch at the right, also the tight bamboo fence at the left.

Changing levels. These simple steps use logs for risers, white gravel for treads. Notice how the stairway makes a turn; also note the bent bamboo guards.

And into the house. One generous cut stone invites the visitor to step up and come in. Notice that the garden fence in the background comes right up to the house.

Garden stones—both natural and cut—in the vendor's yard. The large stone behind the author is 11 feet long, weighs 3 tons.

Lanterns for sale in a Tokyo sales yard. These are antiques, 100 to 500 years old, priced from $138 to $694.

The natural stone lantern at right is only $41; others cost from $500 up. Bridge of cut stone comes to $555.

Nursery trees are grown to near-mature age, then dug up, root-pruned, and delivered to the new garden.

The Japanese garden-maker — and his materials

Almost all Japanese landscape materials are natural materials. The Japanese landscaper shuns lumber and machine-cut stone. He is beginning to use concrete more frequently, but he prefers hand-cut or natural stone. And he builds his fences and gates with bamboo.

For Americans, the Japanese way is expensive. Even in Japan, hand-cut stone for garden paving is costly (see captions). But many similar effects can be achieved in America by using less expensive materials—rough-sawn redwood or cedar, peeled poles, used brick, poured concrete.

A nursery truck delivers a tree with its root-ball roped and bound. Though expensive, trees of this size are prized in Japan.

Tree-transplanting takes place in stages. This tree, already root-balled, is held in the ground until sold, then dug up.

Shaping the tree is nursery practice. The young tree is pruned and trained into more interesting form.

After transplanting, a large tree must be braced against the wind until the roots grow sufficiently to anchor it.

Today the Japanese goes to a garden-supply vendor for gravel and for stone shaped to order. He goes to a nursery for shrubs and trees, which are often moved into his garden in mature size.

A Japanese, if possible, engages a garden-designer—a landscape architect schooled in the traditions of Japanese garden-making and also familiar with today's materials, costs and methods.

The new garden will be man-made all the way. But from the day it is finished it will appear to be complete, and it will suggest nature.

The impression given here is of a woodsy retreat, yet this is a city garden on a busy street. Notice the use of stone with planting in left center.

The Japanese family at home

Japanese families resemble American families in many ways. They enjoy sports and they like to listen to music. They broaden their interests with reading and with travel. They enjoy the privacy of their homes and gardens.

Japanese houses are airy and light—designed with sliding screens called *shoji* which partition the interior space and also open up portions of the outer walls. Floors are covered with a matting called *tatami,* and one removes his shoes when he enters. Within the house are low tables and pillows, no other furniture. At night screens are drawn and bedding is spread directly on the tatami floor. During the day the bedding is folded away.

The shoji screens in the outer walls glide back to open the house to its garden, which is designed to be enjoyed from within the house.

The plan of the typical family-garden goes something like this: Along the borders of the property is some form of fencing or hedge planting to

Screen fencing called *sodegaki* directs the view from indoors toward the planting, lantern and stones outside.

insure privacy from neighbors and from the public street. Usually two gates lead into the entry garden from the street—a smaller gate for the family, a larger gate for visitors. The main garden, reached through the house, is designed to be enjoyed from any point indoors where a shoji can be opened to permit a garden view.

Often the main garden will include a level area, which may be of gravel, beaten earth, or even lawn. Steppingstones provide a pathway from the house into the garden. The planting area meets the open space in an uneven, natural-looking line, with plants graduating in height as they approach the property-line fence or hedge.

A tiny stream may flow around a curve in the planting. The stream may be bridged; there may be a rise in ground level in the rear of the garden; there may be large stones and a tinkling waterfall.

Any unpleasant vista will be shut off with the screening fence called *sodegaki*. Sometimes these fences take off directly from the house wall in such a way that an observer indoors will view only the garden, not another indoor room.

Japanese ideas are changing

To understand the modern Japanese family-garden it is necessary to understand how rapidly Japan is becoming Westernized. Tradition still guides the hand of the garden-designer, but, more and more, tradition is being modified by new ideas.

Today in Japan many people wear Western clothes, eat some Western foods, live in Western-style houses. They drink coffee, eat ice cream, watch television. In fact, they watch American cowboys who speak Japanese. They have modern refrigerators and kitchen ranges. They travel in airplanes and in automobiles. Twenty years ago things were different, but the pace has quickened since the war.

There is still much poverty in Japan. Houses are often small and crowded, and many are quite old. But new houses are going up and new gardens are being installed.

Flower arrangement continues to give much pleasure to the Japanese, but here too I sensed change. Formerly the arrangements were confined to plants locally and seasonally available. The designs usually followed a set style. But now a difference is becoming apparent. No longer must the arranger depend on local materials or be limited by seasonal availability. Flowers from distant areas are on sale in local markets the year around.

Perhaps gardens are changing, too. New gardens are installed very quickly. The feeling of age is there, although a garden crew puts the garden together almost overnight. Materials—stone, plantings, fencing—are transported to the job and assembled. But the new gardens are no less beautiful than the old.

New buildings: Construction goes on everywhere with modern materials and methods, and less handicraft effort.

Changing Japan: TV antennas on the rooftops, Western-style dress, auto traffic, improved street signs and signals.

1. The entrance to a modern garden. A large gate for guests, a small gate for family. Note the tile cap on the garden wall, the neat planting at the base of tree. The steps are broad because the owner likes them that way.

2. The high screen is bamboo reaching above the garden wall. This is an effective way to give a sense of enclosure.

Here is a new Japanese garden

The city garden shown on the next six pages was just six months old when I made my photographs. Camera angles are shown in the sketch plan on the next page.

The owner of this garden, Kenji Kurata, worked out his plans with landscape architect Eijiro Nunokawa. Every decision was made on paper before work began.

3. Inside the gate a neat pathway leads to the house. Delicate, light bamboo planting at right, tall timber bamboo at left.

4. The main garden. The surface is gravel. The pathway beside the house is stone in cement; steppingstones lead out into the garden.

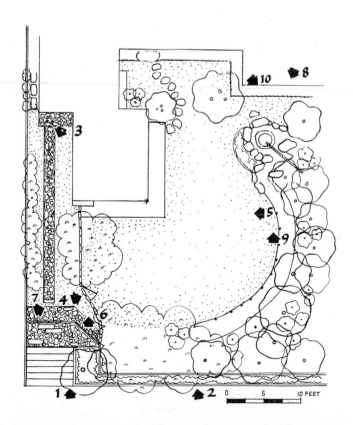

5. An entry fence screens the entry path from the main garden. Note the bamboo grove on both sides of the fence, the steppingstones from gate to house.

29 days and $1,528

What does a modern Japanese garden cost? This one had the following budget:

Trees and other plants	$528
Stone and gravel	389
Fences and gates	110
Labor (including earth moving)	362
	$1,528

The whole job was done by a landscape contractor in just twenty-nine days. When the owner accepted his new garden, it had a finished look, with no signs of newness; actually, with a feeling of age.

6. Continuity is the reason for bamboo planting on both sides. The tall bamboo also serves to interrupt the top line of the fence.

7. The garden gate (see Photo 5) from the entry walk. The gate and fence insure the privacy of the main garden from the entry area.

8. A water basin sits in a corner of the garden, and is fed by a bamboo pipe. Note the stone "stream bed" behind the basin.

Within the main garden

In the large photograph above, only the garden can be seen. Yet to the left is a neighbor's house, and behind the bamboo at the rear is the street.

Here the flat gravel area and the planting area meet. The ground has been built up to a higher level in the planting area. The water basin adds interest, and provides the refreshing sound of falling water. The gravel is *sabijari*—dark, warm red in color.

9. Stones are arranged to suggest a watercourse. There is no water, but the suggestion of water is unmistakable.

10. Fence planting will soften the rigid look of a fence. Some of the planting here rises above the fence to give a sense of continuity.

Here is the Kawamura garden gate from the inside, showing the stepping-stones to the house. Notice the two handles on the gate. One is for luck. The tree has been transplanted recently. It is straw-wrapped to protect against freezing. Stones and planting were kept close to the house corner to give the maximum spaciousness to the garden proper.

Center of interest in the garden

This large rock measures 8 x 4 x 4 feet and weighs about 9 tons. It is the center of interest in a small city garden.

The idea here is to express a feeling of the mountains. Plants and grasses grow in the earth-filled crevices on the top of the rock, softening its strong lines and furthering the impression of a mountain scene.

How the Japanese use screen fences

In Japan a garden fence may be an actual fence, or it may be a wall, a hedge, a screen-planting or a combination of all these. The Motoyoshi Kadokawa garden pictured here contains several good examples of screen fencing.

Above is a privacy fence. Actually it is a bamboo grove inside the property line, with an open bamboo fence behind.

On the next page is a sodegaki or sleeve fence coming out from the house wall. Short bamboo planted in the foreground harmonizes with the fencing.

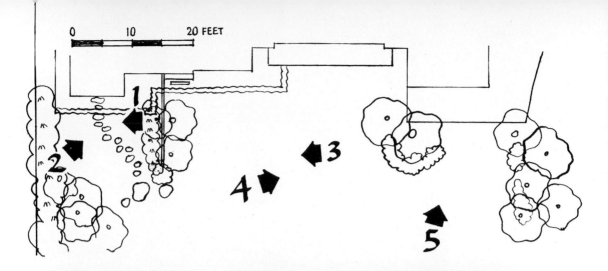

Sometimes fencing . . . sometimes planting

Opposite, above, is a typical sleeve fence extended out into the garden until it merges with a planting area. Notice the change in fence height as it gets farther away from the house.

Opposite, below, is a three-level plant grouping which serves the same purpose as a fence, cutting off the view from the house into one portion of the garden.

Above is the garden in relation to another room in the house. The planting area at the right functions as a privacy screen, but without the stiffness of an actual fence.

A small garden within the garden

Here is Akira Kikkawa's small garden. Just 12 x 20 feet, it is placed at one corner of the house and shows exquisite planning in every detail. Beyond this garden is a larger garden, but all the photographs on these four pages show details of the intimate garden.

1. Looking into the small garden. The short piece of fence and the single pole suggest an entry gate. Steppingstones take the visitor through.

2. (Left) The pathway leading out of the small garden. Note the change in the pathway materials in the photograph and in the plan.

3. (Right) A water basin placed in a rock-lined circular pool close against the screening fence which separates the two gardens.

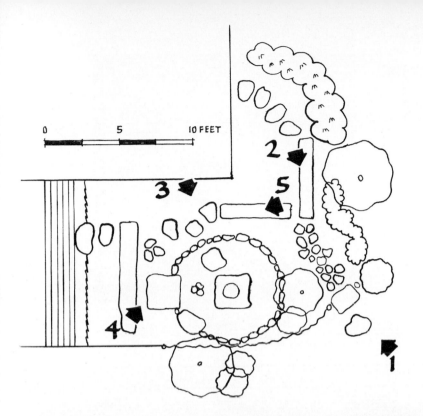

4. Steppingstones. The photographs above and at the right show the careful placement of the steppingstones in Mr. Kikkawa's small garden. A carpet of Japanese moss forms a connecting surface joining the stones.

The purpose of the stones is partly decorative, partly functional. They provide easy and dry walking, but their pattern also offers endless interest.

Notice the careful relationship (here and in the plan on page 41) between the large, rectangular cut stones and the natural boulders connecting them with each other and with the house.

5. Entering the house is simply a matter of stepping up on the last higher stone and onto the strip of decking which runs the full length of the room at floor level. This is a typical arrangement for easy, natural access to and from a garden.

1. *(Above)* A water basin is the center of interest. Notice the privacy fence at the back, the sleeve fence at left, and the careful arrangement of stones and gravel.

A garden to look down upon

Here is another very small garden, just 17 x 20 feet in size. Looking at it, one can easily picture a similar small rectangular area near the entry of an American suburban house or in the side yard near a bedroom or kitchen. Wouldn't a little garden like this be pleasant to look out upon or step out into? This is the Tokyo garden of Takanaru Mitsui.

2. *(Opposite, left)* The water basin rests in a bed of small stones which suggest a creek bed. The large boulders establish the creek bank.

3. *(Opposite, right)* This stone lantern is very old and quite handsome. In the background is a short fence screening from view a small storage area.

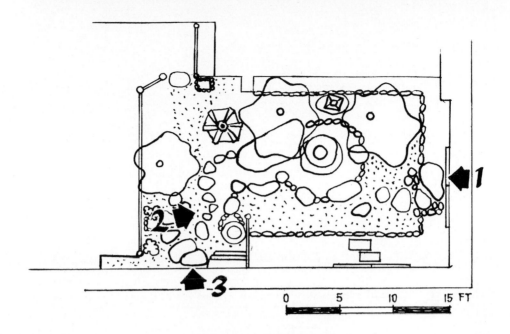

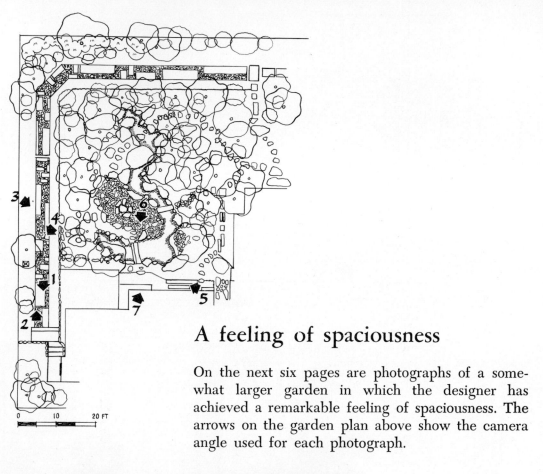

0   10   20 FT

A feeling of spaciousness

On the next six pages are photographs of a somewhat larger garden in which the designer has achieved a remarkable feeling of spaciousness. The arrows on the garden plan above show the camera angle used for each photograph.

1. *(Left)* From the house one steps down into the garden by means of broad stone steps which change dimension in an interesting way. This variation helps to give the illusion of distance from the garden gate.

2. *(Right)* A straight paved path, very trim and tailored, made with both cut and natural stone set in cement, leads into the garden. Notice the neat screen fence at the right. Note, also, how the path turns, beckoning the visitor to explore what lies around the bend.

3. Side entrance to the garden (see plan) leads around the end of a screen fence and up a gentle rise of steppingstones, passing a water basin on the way.

The owner of this garden, Eijiro Nunokawa, is himself a landscape architect, as were his father and grandfather before him. In his own garden he wished to suggest a mountain scene with a spacious approach to the mountain woodland.

Mr. Nunokawa built his house in the far corner of his lot, with a pathway

4. Beside the path is a striking Ishitoro standing alone as a garden decoration. Beside it, growing at the foot of a tree, is a single luxuriant aralia (*Fatsia japonica*).

to the house along one side of the lot. The ground on one side of the path is elevated to supply background for the garden. From the house one can look out upon a creek crossed by two bridges.

Turn the page for more photographs of Eijiro Nunokawa's garden.

5. View from the house (see plan). The bridge is a stone slab, with stone paving beyond. The pathway shown in Photo No. 2 appears behind the screen fence at the left.

6. The stone bridge is flanked by an upright stone of the same length, so placed as to give a sense of safety and to add design interest.

7. Mr. Nunokawa's garden! Over 500 plants were used, all indigenous to a mountainous locality. They are planted in such a way that the garden appears to rise from the foreground, with a mountain brook flowing down through the boulders. The mountain effect is further heightened by the songs of the caged birds which hang in the garden trees.

Long, narrow entry garden

Takeo Manabe's entry garden is a study in simplicity. Mr. Manabe wanted his garden to have a feeling of age, and so he used bamboo. How well a neat and straightforward approach like this would go with a contemporary American house!

1. *(Below)* A long straight walk leads from the street to the house.

2. Open bamboo fencing on the property line, with shrub planting behind and grass planting at the base of the fence.

3. Three stone slabs interrupt the long line of the entry walk. Notice the straight lines in this garden. Not all Japanese gardens are completely "natural" designs.

The garden gate

4. *(Left)* The main gate, closed. At the right is a low door for family use. Notice the repetition of the pathway stone pattern at the base of the gate structure.

5. The gate, open. The pathway jogs right toward the house. Now in view is a mixed planting of bamboo and maples.

6. Garden entry to the house. When new shoots of bamboo spring up, the owner studies them closely. A few that improve the setting are retained but most are dug up. The garden floor is natural soil.

1. A cluster of bamboo grows on both sides of the fence (see plan, page 59).

This is a bamboo garden

The photographs above were taken from the house porch at points twenty-five feet apart. The contrast between the sparse and dense bamboo plantings adds to the interest of this simple garden.

This is the favorite garden of Choka Adachi, who designed it himself.

2. The stone lantern and water basin are set in a bamboo grove. Note pathway.

Mr. Adachi conducts the Tokyo Kagei school of flower-arranging, draws and paints and is a professional photographer. In addition, he is a good fisherman, and I can vouch for the fact that he is a good cook.

For more photographs and a plan of Choka Adachi's bamboo garden, turn the page.

3. Seventeen bamboo make up this single group planting close to the house. Mr. Adachi's garden demonstrates a quite typical Japanese treatment of the garden floor. For the most part it is natural soil and gravel. The pathway stones break the level surface and keep one's feet from getting wet and muddy in rainy weather.

4. *(Opposite, above)*. Fence intersection. One fence is higher than the other, and the height of the gateposts varies proportionately. The high fence extends a short distance into the garden beyond the line of the gate. Back of these fences is a second garden planted both in deciduous and evergreen trees and shrubs.

5. *(Opposite, below)*. Pathway. As the pathway approaches the house, its character changes. At the end are three rectangular cut stones; then two stone blocks function as steps leading up to floor level.

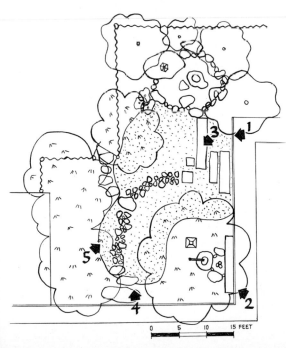

0   5   10   15 FEET

1. This entry pathway typically avoids a straight line yet is easy to follow. The garden floor is gravel, neatly raked.

Steppingstones on gravel

The home of Mr. and Mrs. Takanaru Mitsui is surrounded by gardens. Their central garden was pictured on pages 44 and 45.

The entrance above uses three rectangular, paved slabs—small stones set in concrete. These slabs are the size and shape of the tatami mats used as indoor floor-covering in Japanese houses. Since in Japan one always removes his shoes before entering the house onto the tatami mats, these slabs are a suggestion of welcome.

More photographs and the garden plan are on pages 62 and 63.

2. Natural stone pathway. The pathway may give the impression of a hit-or-miss arrangement, but the placement of each stone was most carefully considered. The stones lead to the main garden. The house entrance is at the right.

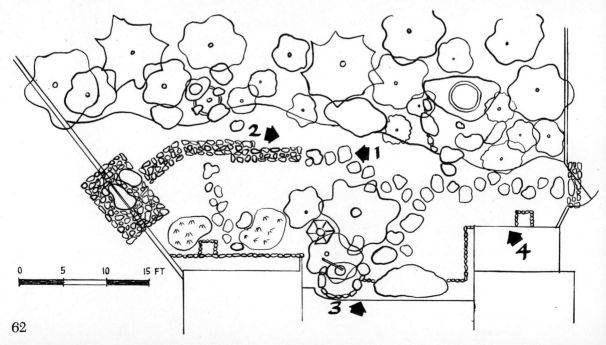

3. *(Opposite page)* Here is one view from inside the house. The placement of the stones carries the eye along to points of interest, such as the water basin set back among evergreen shrubs. The stones also lead out of sight to the right, suggesting undiscovered pleasures just around the corner.

4. *(Above)* Here is the water basin close up. Its design is unusual—a circular basin cut in a large, irregular stone. Surrounding the basin is an area of small stones, and then shrub planting intermixed with stone lanterns and small maples.

3. Looking toward the entrance. Compare this with Photo No. 2 on page 65. The paving stones are raised above the earth level here. Notice that the tree and shrub areas are well separated.

4. Another view of the approach walk. The planting area fits neatly within the curve of the walk. A Japanese garden-maker would understand the famous statement of architect Mies Van der Rohe, "Less is more." Gardens like this one achieve their spacious feeling by being uncrowded. Simplicity and restraint are the keynotes.

1. Square steppingstones lead to a large circular pool, which is quite formal in its placement (see plan).

A Japanese garden, "Western style"

Landscape architects Kodo Matsubara and Motonosuke Shibata, who designed this modern garden for Kiyoshi Kakimoto, consider it a Western-style design. To American eyes it is still a Japanese garden, but it differs markedly from some of the gardens in earlier pages.

The stone placement here is mathematically precise, with none of the studied irregularity typical of Japanese landscape practice. Instead of the usual water basin, there is a modern container on black steel legs. The 15 x 20 inch paving stones make two precise right-angle turns on their way to the pool garden.

3. The taking-off-shoes stone at the house entrance (see text below).

Mr. Kakimoto's modern garden is less "natural" than a traditional garden. One sees no Ishitoro, no water basin. The planting is more lush than severe.

Yet at least one traditional essential is here—the large stone at the doorstep (Photos 2 and 3). In Japan all rooms opening into the garden have such stone steps, which are called *Kutsunugi ishi*. *Kutsu* means shoe; *nugi* means

4. These accent stones are set in a planting area of azaleas.

off; *ishi* is stone. So these are taking-off-shoes stones.

Although rooms opening to the garden have access to these stones, the Kutsunugi ishi sometimes have only a decorative function. The same is true of water basins. They are not necessarily functional, even though they do contain water.

1. *(Left)* View from the gate entrance. The stone slabs set lengthwise give a feeling of depth.

Plan: The entry garden runs parallel to the street. Notice how fencing confines the entry area. The street-side fence is straight; the garden-side fence makes no less than seven bends.

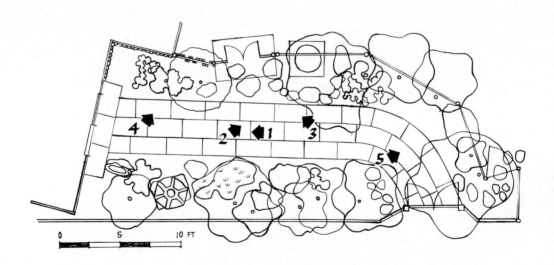

2. Water overflows the basin, covering the stones below to a depth of about three inches, then flows behind the basin and on to a pool in another part of the garden.

The entry garden welcomes the guest

Mr. and Mrs. Giichi Miura wanted the approach to their house to be indirect, with an entry garden that would interest the arriving guest. On the right (see plan) is a water basin, an arrangement of natural stones, and an inner gate to the main family garden. The left side of the garden is of less interest, although it is well planted and contains a lantern.

3. *(Left)* Garden gate. With its gable roof and solid structure, the gate emphasizes the enclosed nature of the garden.

4. *(Below)* The sleeve fence is made of Japanese bush clover *(tepo gaki)* bound in bundles. Note the pattern: 3-2-3-1-2-3-3. The fence roof prevents water from draining on the tepo gaki. The tree is a Maki *(Podocarpus macrophylla)*.

5. The rock in the fence. Here is a garden detail that is typically Japanese. Giichi Miura and his landscape architect, Motonosuke Shibata, gave this corner of the entry garden a great deal of thought. The large rock is the key. It measures 4 x 4 x 6 feet. About 70 per cent of its bulk is on this side of the fence; the rest extends into the main garden which lies behind the fence. The old pomegranate in the foreground is permitted to keep some of its new growth to add to the composition. The fence itself is partially a "see-through." The visitor's eye can follow the surface of the ground and sense the garden beyond.

1. Approach to the teahouse. Crossing the path is a solid, four-panel gate, attached to a short sleeve fence which joins the teahouse.

The tea garden — elegant simplicity

Giishi Miura's teahouse is located well away from his main house and has its own garden. Both teahouse and garden are quite small; they are designed in the traditional way and contain the necessary equipment for the Tea ceremony.

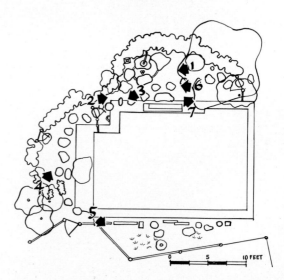

76

2. Entering the teahouse. The Kutsunugi ishi (taking-off-shoes stone) is unusual. A rectangular cut-stone is flanked on two sides with small natural stones set in concrete. The Kutsunugi ishi measures 10 x 12 x 48 inches.

The large photograph shows the approach path and the entrance to the teahouse. The large, vertical bamboo is actually a water pipe carrying water from the roof. The other large tree is a persimmon. Out of the picture to the left is the water basin.

For more photographs of this tea garden turn the page.

3. (Above) Close-up of the gate area. The steppingstones rest in a carpet of clean white gravel. The group of black stones is a drainage device.

4. (Right) The teahouse gate. Just beyond is the Ishitoro, placed to light the path for the visitor. A second, taller lantern can be seen further along.

5. Garden detail (see plan for location). An ancient lantern surrounded by ten bamboo, and two natural stones for decoration. The fence here is 7 feet high.

6. Water basin. In the center is a stone to stand on. On the left is the stone on which to set the lantern; on the right, the stone for the water container. The Tea ritual has a strictly set pattern, and the arrangement here is traditional.

7. A bamboo pipe fills the water basin; water is dipped out with the bamboo dipper. The white gravel ground-cover is used to suggest cleanliness.

The idea is privacy. The wall is high and sturdy; so is the gate.

The fence roof. There's a practical reason; it keeps rain off the fence.

Japanese gardens are fenced gardens

Japanese gardens make use of two quite different kinds of fencing. Along property lines are partition fences, sturdily built. I *call* them fences here, but sometimes they actually are masonry or concrete walls, or dense hedges, or combinations of wall and hedge, fence and hedge, or wall and fence.

Within the garden are *sodegaki*—sleeve fences or screen fences. These are usually lightly constructed. Their purpose is to divide the garden, to direct the eye and the footstep, to separate the views, often to obscure an unwanted view. The sodegaki are usually low and usually short.

Gates correspond to the fences. Those in the outer fence may be as sturdy as the wall itself. Gates within the garden are often lightly built.

At the entry there are usually two gates. The larger gate is for guests; the small, low gate, for the family (you have to duck your head).

A roofed gate in a garden fence.

A minimum fence and a minimum gate.

A fence-hedge is a popular device. This is the public or street side. Pruning maintains an even top line, but the general effect is neat without being rigidly formal.

Fences are used as windbreaks and also, frequently, for visual privacy— to shut off a view of a neighbor's roof, for example.

The high fence on page 83 is an interesting example. Giishi Miura chose this lofty fence because he wanted privacy from his neighbor and also a backdrop for his garden.

This fence begins with a 7-foot concrete wall. Rising above it another 12 feet is a latticework of bamboo in 1-foot squares. Three feet in front of the fence Mr. Miura planted Japanese evergreen oaks. These have been pruned and trained in an informal espalier through the high lattice work. In time Mr. Miura expects to have a solid, leafy-green hedge 19 feet tall!

In the United States we have many trees which can be trained to produce a similar effect. Ask your local nurseryman to suggest which trees would serve well in your climate area.

(Above) The sodegaki here provides a background for the rock garden. Extending from the house, it shields from view the area behind the rock garden.

(Left) Sodegaki and gate. The short fence is made with dried bark and poles. The gate is a simple one—boards held together with battens at right angles. Notice that the battens extend above the boards.

(*Left*) Natural path. Stones are set so that they look like nature's work.

(*Below*) Stream bed path. The gravel suggests a watercourse. It warns you to follow the steppingstones to avoid getting wet.

Path and steps. Stones set in concrete form the path. The steps are simply four large stones rising in elevation.

The garden pathway

The Japanese are at their most creative in the design of garden pathways. Although they prefer stone, natural or uncut, and seldom use such Western favorites as asphalt and concrete, many of their path designs are quite adaptable to American conditions.

The Japanese path does more than get one to his destination. It guides the footsteps along a route planned for maximum appreciation of the garden. And the path itself is often one of the strongest elements of the garden's design. On the next few pages are close-ups of a variety of pathways.

(Above) Log path. This rustic walk is decorative, and deliberately so. The walk is of Kuri logs, about 18 inches in length, set unevenly with about two-thirds of each log embedded in the earth. Note the smaller logs hammered into the earth to hold the stepping logs in place.

(Opposite, above) Stone walk. In contrast to the rustic log path, this elegant walk uses stone cut in squares and cut-stone borders. Flanking the walk is a surface of raked gravel.

(Opposite, below) Broken stone. This path uses many sizes and colors of stone, assembled carefully in a harmonious composition. The gentle curve is deliberate; it adds interest.

Steps...interesting and functional

A Japanese garden seldom has the formal steps Americans know so well. There are so many other and more interesting ways to get up or down a slope! As you can see here, the materials can be almost anything. Often as not, the steps may simply be a sequence of large stones set into a slope. And, as Japanese garden-makers (usually, but not always) avoid stiff architectural lines, the steps will curve just as the garden pathways do.

Stone steps *(above)* flanked on one side by larger stones, on the other by a planted bank. Earth steps *(opposite)* with slim log risers secured by stakes. Again, note the gentle curve.

Floating stones *(opposite, above)*. Steps in natural stone lead up the slope. But they travel uphill in a broader course of small stones set in earth.

Formal stair *(opposite, below)*. The steps are even, the edging on the left side is formal; but consider the right side—natural stone and planting.

Gentle slope *(above)*. Here is a side path, rising slowly. The garden-maker used broad treads of gravel with shallow log risers. The effect is so easy and informal one hardly realizes he is climbing.

The gateway *(left)* is formed by two offset sleeve fences. The stones guide one's footsteps through the gateway and also contribute to the over-all design.

A flat stone *(below)* with a planting of short bamboo along one side makes a point of interest in a garden lawn.

A combination of stone and planting. This large stone is literally recessed within a planting area. It becomes the dominant design element in the grouping.

Stone as garden decoration

Every Japanese garden uses stone in one form or another. Sometimes the stone has a precise functional or decorative role—as a path, as steps, as a bridge, as an Ishitoro or a water basin. But just as often the stone is used in combination with planting, or in combinations of stone, to suggest a natural scene.

Cylinders *(left)* of carved stone make an unusual and effective garden decoration.

This tower *(below)* of six stones has the shape and general character of a stone lantern.

A stone lantern placed at a garden entrance, with low azalea and large natural stone at its base.

Decorative stone in the garden

Originally stone lanterns were used in Japanese gardens as lights to illuminate the pathway to the teahouse. Today they are largely ornamental. The modern trend, sometimes, is to use too many of them, or to use lanterns too large in scale for their surroundings. Where more than one lantern is used, each one usually differs in design and in setting.

A lantern is customarily placed near the water basin; one needs light to wash his hands before entering the teahouse for the Tea ceremony.

An ornamental iron lantern can be both decorative and practical; this one is used as a garden light. Azaleas are planted between the stones at its base. The garden corner shown here, designed by landscape architect Eijiro Nunokawa, had been installed just one month at the time the photograph was made.

A hanging lantern in ornamental iron is suspended from the eave. Lanterns of this type are made in a wide variety of designs and are frequently used for garden illumination. Notice the bamboo screen which shields the crawl space under the building; also the bamboo roll blinds above the wall opening.

The place of the water basin

In today's family-garden in Japan the water basin is usually used for decoration, although occasionally it will play its role in the Tea ceremony. These basins can be seen in endless variety—made from a single hollowed stone, or from a series of stone slabs. They may be filled manually, or fed from an overhead bamboo pipe, or fed from below.

Above is a lovely round basin, very old, placed on an irregular natural stone, with a few ferns growing at the base.

Opposite is a simple stone basin mounted dramatically on a stone support and placed conveniently beside the veranda.

Water basins...in almost endless variety

The water basin can take many forms, as the photographs here demonstrate.

Opposite are four quite different basins. At top left is a very large basin approached over steppingstones. The one at top right is a ceramic basin used inside the house. At lower left is a heavy, square basin formed by cementing together four stone slabs. The basin at lower right, with a stone lantern close by, is made of hollowed stone.

The almost cylindrical basin in the photograph above is interesting. It is placed close to the veranda with an additional porch area built out to suggest easy access. Note the floor track to guide the sliding shoji screens.

The suggestion of water...a sea of sand

The photographs here show one of the most celebrated of all Japanese gardens—the temple garden of Ryoan-ji in Kyoto. People interested in garden design come from all parts of Japan to visit Ryoan-ji.

Centuries old, the garden is simply a rectangle of carefully raked white sand, enclosed in a beautiful tile-roofed plaster wall. There are no trees or other major plantings, but the garden contains fifteen stones arranged in groupings of two, three, and five—five groupings in all, with moss growing at the base of the groupings.

What does this garden suggest? It is a sea of sand, with a few islands thrusting up above the water.

The suggestion of water...a rippling creek

Just as a stream finds its way downhill, widening as it reaches level ground, so does the dry watercourse above. It starts as a narrow rivulet trickling over rough rocks. As it moves down it widens over a bed of smaller water-washed stones, with heavy boulders on the banks at either side.

There is not a drop of water flowing in this little creek. Yet who can mistake its suggestion of a cool, rippling stream?

(*Above*) Here is a dry garden pond. Polished black pebbles are the "water!" Larger, irregular stones form the "banks." And the steppingstones of the pathway provide a dry crossing.

(*Left*) A garden pathway crosses this tiny watercourse made of 2-inch stones.

Stone steps lead down to the water's edge.

The suggestion of water...

These photographs show three more ways in which the Japanese garden-maker uses stone to suggest a water-course or garden pond.

(Opposite, above) The bank of a rock-bordered stream. The large flat stone suggests a place where the visitor can kneel beside the creek and trail his hand in the water.

(Opposite, below) The shore of this pond is so natural-looking one suspects it may have been only temporarily drained. The water will surely be back tomorrow!

A pool, flanked by beautiful natural stone, extends under the veranda of the house.

The place of water in the garden

A Japanese garden is not complete without water. In suggesting a natural scene, the garden-maker will use waterfalls, streams, and ponds—if he can. But ponds are not always possible, and waterfalls are difficult to design properly and expensive to install. Hence the garden-maker often has to be content with only the "suggestion" of water, as shown in the photographs on the preceding pages.

But the photographs here show ways in which the garden-maker does introduce real water into his garden scheme.

(Right) A mere trickle wets the face of a large natural stone.

(Below) The back of the stone shown above. Notice the pipe which supplies the trickle. A faucet controls the flow.

A rough stone conceals the spray nozzle in a garden pond.

Two stones conceal the spray nozzle in this pond.

With a spray...the coolness of summer rain

In many modern Japanese gardens a fine mist spray or a more powerful jet spray is used to cool the garden in summer.

In this photograph an adjustable fountain spray shoots up above the steppingstone pathway. The water falls back into the pool, and is drained off to maintain a constant level a few inches below the surface of the steppingstones. Note the veranda entry at the left. This is the Kobe garden of Mr. Kinjiro Yamamoto.

Water at two levels with a short waterfall between.

The sound of falling water

It does not take much of a fall, or a large volume of water, to create the pleasant and natural effect of a waterfall. The two garden pools on different levels pictured above are joined by a slowly trickling waterfall. A small rock dam controls the water flow.

On the opposite page is a simple but decorative waterfall. A small stream falls from rocks concealed behind the mixed planting of *Fatsia japonica* and azaleas. The polished white, black and gray pebbles below are kept wet by the little waterfall.

A water pathway. Notice the stepping-off stone, the very large stone midway, and then the three steppingstones beyond.

When you walk across water

The Japanese garden-designer achieves some of his most pleasant effects in the manner in which he guides one's footsteps across water.

Often as not he employs steppingstones. And in spite of their apparently almost haphazard placement, the stones are easy to walk upon and spaced just right for a convenient and safe crossing.

Opposite is a house built beside a pond. The steppingstones trace a broad curve with one zigzag halfway along.

A zigzag bridge of rough planking. This off-center design is quite typical, as are the post and beam supports.

The garden footbridge

A Japanese garden bridge may be natural in appearance, or frankly man-made of cut stone or timbers. Often some element—a stone or post or a tall planting—marks the edge of the bridge and thus gives you a sense of safety. This warning device is usually handled in such a natural way that your steps are guided, yet you may not be aware of the caution that is part of the bridge design.

This stone-slab bridge has a center stone support. Often this type of bridge is designed off-center like the wooden bridge on the opposite page.

The bridge approach here is marked by steppingstones. The large stones at the bridge corners are decorative and give a feeling of security.

The point of interest

Many unusual objects are displayed in Japanese gardens—in this case, a large rounded stone, white in color, with a smooth surface. The surrounding planting has been clipped to conceal the base of the stone but reveal its upper part, and also to silhouette the stone from one side.

This is just an abstract arrangement within the garden, but what might it suggest to the imaginative eye?

The power of suggestion

Here is a mound of sand, roughly conical but with a flat top. In many sand gardens a mound of this type, but smaller, adds interest to the otherwise unrelieved sand area.

What does this mound suggest? Mount Fuji, perhaps. But it may also suggest the silvery moon to the viewer who looks down on the mound from the pavilion above.

Stone decoration. Today's garden-designers in Japan like to experiment. The decoration shown above has no traditional purpose—just two stone cylinders with an X connection, also in stone. The bent bamboo edging is often used along pathways.

(*Above*) A log stump is this garden-owner's choice for an unusual garden ornament. It is his own idea and he is highly pleased with it.

(*Left*) The design of the water basin is an enlarged version of a Japanese coin.

A log pathway leads to the stone lantern placed by the garden wall. This pathway is not really functional, but it attracts the eye and draws it to the lantern and the surrounding planting.

Simplicity is an attribute of Japanese design. This new garden uses a gravel ground-cover, cherry trees, an azalea planting by the fence. The owner has hung a favorite hat on the outside wall.

The planting in Japanese gardens

In this book I have purposely emphasized the elements of design and have refrained from discussing the planting in detail.

While the majority of the plants most frequently used in Japanese gardens are available in the United States, I do not think it advisable to copy Japanese gardens literally in this country. We have dozens of shrubs and trees that give similar effects and that perform well in our climate.

Here, however, is a brief summing-up of the Japanese garden-maker's approach to planting, including a short listing of some of the plants most commonly used in Japanese gardens.

First of all, the Japanese gardener plants with restraint. He may use only three or four kinds of shrubs, and perhaps just one or two kinds of trees. Or he may do a garden around a single beautiful pine!

Next, the Japanese designer tries for spaciousness. He avoids the crowding of plants; he gives them plenty of room.

Although the designer uses deciduous trees and shrubs, he frames his garden in evergreens. He grows no annuals or perennials in the main garden, but he may have them elsewhere in a cutting garden.

He prizes moss and likes to use stone with surface breaks and crevices that will encourage moss. He likes ferns and plants them near water.

The Japanese garden-designer tries to combine plants that are found together in nature. He avoids mixtures from seacoast and mountain; he avoids combinations from widely different climates. And he is not afraid to use his pruning shears. Plants are thinned, cut back, shaped, contorted— but they are not left alone. Growth is guided to achieve the desired effect, and the garden is kept from becoming crowded and overgrown.

Here are a few of the plants most often used:

Japanese maple; flowering cherry, crab apple, plum and quince; pines— especially the Japanese black pine and red pine; bamboo; oak; deciduous magnolia; ginkgo; holly; juniper.

Also: gardenia, daphne, camellia, azalea, rhododendron, aucuba, nandina, mondo grass, wisteria, aralia, Japanese and Siberian iris.

Colors in the Japanese garden are subtle—the greens and grays of foliage, the young buds of spring and the yellows and crimsons of autumn. Flowering and berried shrubs and flowering trees add vivid color in season.